DOES THE 21st CENTURY
BELONG TO
CHINA?

DOES THE 21st CENTURY
BELONG TO
CHINA?

KISSINGER AND ZAKARIA VS. FERGUSON AND LI

THE MUNK DEBATE ON CHINA

EDITED BY RUDYARD GRIFFITHS AND PATRICK LUCIANI

ANANSI

This edition published in 2011 by
House of Anansi Press Inc.
110 Spadina Avenue, Suite 801
Toronto, ON, M5V 2K4
Tel. 416-363-4343
Fax 416-363-1017
www.anansi.ca

Distributed in Canada by
HarperCollins Canada Ltd.
1995 Markham Road
Scarborough, ON, M1B 5M8
Toll free tel. 1-800-387-0117

Distributed in the United States by
Publishers Group West
1700 Fourth Street
Berkeley, CA 94710
Toll free tel. 1-800-788-3123

House of Anansi Press is committed to protecting our natural environment.
As part of our efforts, this book is printed on paper that contains 100%
post-consumer recycled fibres, is acid-free, and is processed chlorine-free.

15 14 13 12 11   1 2 3 4 5

LIBRARY AND ARCHIVES CANADA CATALOGUING IN PUBLICATION

Does the 21st century belong to China? : the Munk
debate on China / Henry Kissinger ... [et al.] ; edited by
Rudyard Griffiths and Patrick Luciani.

(The Munk debates)
ISBN 978-1-77089-062-6

1. China — History — 21st century. I. Kissinger, Henry,
1923– II. Griffiths, Rudyard III. Luciani, Patrick
IV. Series: Munk debates

DS779.4.D63 2011   951.06   C2011-904008-5

Library of Congress Control Number: 2011929943

Cover design and typesetting: Alysia Shewchuk
Text design: Colleen Wormald
Transcription: Rondi Adamson

Canada Council   Conseil des Arts   ONTARIO ARTS COUNCIL
for the Arts   du Canada   CONSEIL DES ARTS DE L'ONTARIO

*We acknowledge for their financial support of our publishing program the
Canada Council for the Arts, the Ontario Arts Council, and the Government of
Canada through the Canada Book Fund.*

Printed and bound in Canada

CONTENTS

INTRODUCTION BY PETER MUNK

On the evening of June 17, 2011, we held our seventh Munk Debate at Toronto's Roy Thomson Hall. The auditorium, which seats 2,700, was filled to capacity, and there were thousands of people following the debate online. It was thrilling for me to be part of an event that in only three years has captured a wide and growing audience across Canada and beyond.

When we started holding these debates three years ago, it was our intention to bring the best minds to Toronto to grapple with some crucial issues facing the world. Our goal was to elevate the quality of discussion on important global matters for the benefit of Canadians. I am proud to say that through the work and efforts of the Aurea Foundation Board we have been able to achieve this, and here I especially want to credit Rudyard Griffiths for his vision and management. On June 17 he once again acted as host and moderator of the debate.

I have always believed that clarity is best achieved by inviting the finest thinkers to speak to us when they do not see eye-to-eye. There is nothing wrong with describing and discussing crucial issues, but debating them is better. The world is no different from any other object in that we can make more sense of it by viewing it from different angles.

I think the best way to achieve this clarity is through a format that challenges informed and articulate thinkers to go beyond telling us what they know, or think they know. Talking about the times in which we live is one thing, but to stand up and defend ideas when they are being challenged by equally informed and articulate opponents who think they know better, is another. Which was what the debaters did on the evening of June 17 at Roy Thomson Hall. The topic was China. We in the West have traditionally focused on the Near East, and understandably so, but the last two decades compelled us to increasingly turn our attention to the Far East. China has seemingly come out of nowhere to play an important economic and political role around the world. It wasn't out of nowhere, of course. China's growth started with the country's shift to the market economy in 1978. Even taking this shift into account, an average growth of 10 percent per annum by the early 1990s was so impressive as to seem aberrant or unreal. With new-found economic strength, and especially since they gained this strength at a time when Europe and the United States were perceived to be losing theirs, China has also taken its place on the international stage as a leading political power.

The debate in Toronto was about determining whether or not China will be able to sustain that momentum and become the dominant global force of the 21st century.

We were privileged to have four of the most insightful thinkers on the subject. First, I felt truly humbled to introduce Dr. Henry Kissinger, who had graciously accepted our invitation to participate. There isn't much I could say about Dr. Kissinger that readers wouldn't already know. He is not only a brilliant student and teacher of history, but more importantly, he is a maker of history. We remember him for his role in opening up China for the West when he was a member of President Richard Nixon's cabinet as Secretary of State. He received the Nobel Peace Prize in 1973 for his extraordinary work on the international stage, and he received the Presidential Medal of Freedom in 1977.

That evening we were witnessing a bit of history as well. I learned that Dr. Kissinger had never taken part in a public debate, so this really was a special occasion and an honour for all of us at The Munk Debates. He came to Toronto following the recent publication of his monumental book, *On China*, and was arguing against the resolution.

Joining Dr. Kissinger was the young rising international star: Fareed Zakaria. I am sure most readers have seen Fareed as the host of *Fareed Zakaria: GPS*, CNN's flagship program on international affairs. Named by *Foreign Policy* as one of the top 100 global thinkers, he is also the editor-at-large for *Time* magazine, and the author of a number of books, including the bestsellers

The Future of Freedom and *The Post-American World.* At the age of twenty-eight he was editor of the prestigious journal *Foreign Affairs.* He then went on to *Newsweek,* where he wrote a number of award-winning articles, including his famous October 2001 piece, "The Politics of Rage: Why Do They Hate Us?" And last year Fareed earned an Emmy nomination for his interview with China's Premier Wen Jiabao.

Arguing for the resolution was Niall Ferguson, who took part in the first Munk Debate in 2008. Not only is Professor Ferguson a distinguished economic historian at Harvard University, he is also the bestselling author of numerous books. His latest, entitled *Civilization: The West and the Rest,* will be published in North America in November 2011.

Professor Ferguson's understanding of the world economy is made accessible by his skills in bringing that knowledge to a wide audience. Recognizing the key factors that drive economic growth, his thesis was that China possesses all that is necessary to propel it to international pre-eminence. What added special piquancy to the evening was that Professor Ferguson is Dr. Kissinger's official biographer.

I also welcomed Dr. David Daokui Li, who joined Niall on the pro side. Not only does he know intimately the factors that have made China an economic powerhouse, he also brought a unique perspective and personal knowledge of China. His childhood was spent in Sichuan province, as a result of his parents being displaced to the countryside during the Cultural Revolution. Under such conditions he managed to earn his doctorate in economics at Harvard University and currently holds a number of teaching positions in the United States and in his home country. He is the Director of the Center for China in the World Economy at the Tsinghua University School of Economics and Management in Beijing. He is also a delegate to the Beijing People's Congress, one of three academic members of the monetary policy committee of the Central Bank of China, and a member of the World Economic Forum in Davos.

I'm certain that you'll enjoy this printed version of these exciting few hours.

Peter Munk
Founder, the Aurea Foundation
Toronto, July 2011

Does the 21st Century Belong to China?

Pro: Niall Ferguson and David Li
Con: Henry Kissinger and Fareed Zakaria

June 17, 2011
Toronto, Canada

THE MUNK DEBATE ON CHINA

RUDYARD GRIFFITHS: Ladies and gentlemen, welcome to Roy Thomson Hall in Toronto, Canada. We are here for the Munk Debate on China. My name is Rudyard Griffiths, I'm the co-organizer of the Munk Debates along with my colleague, Patrick Luciani, and it is my privilege to be your moderator once again.

First, I want to welcome the thousands of people watching this debate online, live on the Internet, on globeandmail.com and munkdebates.com. It's terrific to have you as a part of these proceedings. A warm hello also to the millions of people watching, reading, and listening to this debate, everywhere from the Australian Broadcasting Corporation down under to C-SPAN throughout the United States, to the People's Daily Online in China, and through our international media partnership with the *Financial Times* of London and its prestigious China Confidential research unit.

Hello, too, to Canadians coast-to-coast, who are listening and watching everywhere from CBC Radio's *Ideas* program to the Canadian Public Affairs Channel (CPAC), and on the network where I host a daily television show, Business News Network (BNN). It's great to have you as part of this debate. And finally, as I look around this hall, which is filled to capacity, I'd like to welcome the 2,700 people who have come out for a second time for the Munk Debates at Roy Thomson Hall.

Everyone associated with this project thanks you for your support for the simple idea behind this series, which is dedicated to creating opportunities like this, where we can debate the big geopolitical issues that are changing Canada and changing the world. The success of this debate series, its ability to bring to Toronto some of the world's sharpest thinkers, would not be possible without the philanthropic creativity and generosity of two individuals. I'd like all of you to join me in a round of applause for our hosts, the co-founders of the Munk Debates, Peter and Melanie Munk. Bravo you two. We're going to keep at this.

Now, for the moment we have all been waiting for. We have the motion before us: Be it resolved the 21st century will belong to China; now, all we need is our debaters centre stage. Let's have a big round of applause for the two debaters who will be arguing for the motion, Niall Ferguson and David Li. Now, let's welcome their formidable opponents, Fareed Zakaria and Dr. Henry Kissinger.

Niall Ferguson is well known to those familiar with the Munk Debates. During the first debate in 2008, he and

Charles Krauthammer bested current National Security Council member Samantha Power and the late Richard Holbrooke on the motion: Be it resolved the world is a safer place with a Republican in the White House. That was a very spirited debate. Since 2008, Niall Ferguson has added to his raft of internationally best-selling books with the publication of *The Ascent of Money: A Financial History of the World* and *Civilization: The West and the Rest.* He holds a variety of prestigious professorships and lectureships everywhere from Oxford University to Harvard University to the London School of Economics. Ladies and gentlemen, welcome Niall Ferguson.

Our next debater joins us from Beijing, China, where he is the director of the Center for China in the World Economy at the Tsinghua University School of Economics and Management in Beijing. In many ways his personal biography mirrors China's rise. His family was displaced by the Cultural Revolution; David has memories of this, although he was only a four-year-old boy. Twenty-eight years later he received a Ph.D. from Harvard University. He is now one of only three academic members of the Monetary Policy Advisory Committee of the Central Bank of China. One indication of the key role that he plays representing a new generation of thought leadership in China is this: David, an economist, has more than three million followers on the Chinese equivalent of Twitter.

Fareed Zakaria is familiar to many Canadians. He's the host and the driving force behind CNN's flagship international affairs program, *Fareed Zakaria: GPS*. You have also read his column in *Time* magazine, where he is editor-at-large, and he writes for the *Washington Post.* He is the author of the internationally acclaimed books *The Future of Freedom: Illiberal Democracy at Home and Abroad* and the recently updated *Post-American World: Release 2.0.* As you will hear during this debate, Fareed is one of today's most thoughtful and provocative U.S. thinkers on America's role in the world and the effect of rising international powers. Fareed Zakaria, it is a pleasure to have you here.

Our final debater has played a central role in global affairs for the last half-century. He has been honoured with the Nobel Peace Prize for his public service, and he was presented with the Presidential Medal of Freedom. He is the single individual here today who can interpret China's rise, given his unique contribution to bringing China back into the community of nations after its Cultural Revolution. And, participating in his first public debate on China or any other subject, he makes history again. Ladies and gentlemen, please welcome to the Munk Debates the 56th secretary of state of the United States, Dr. Henry Kissinger.

Now, let's briefly run through how the debate will unfold. Each of our debaters will have six minutes for their opening statements to make their case for and against the motion. After the opening statements, we're going to have our debaters cross-examine each other's views and opinions, and then we're going to bring the audience into the conversation. We will have questions from notable people in the audience, which incudes students from the Munk School of Global Affairs, and finally we will have a raft of questions from our own web site, Facebook, and Twitter, which I will weave into the conversation.

So how did the audience vote before coming into this debate? Did you believe the 21st century will belong to China? The numbers are interesting: 39 percent believe the century could be owned by China, 40 percent voted against the motion, and 21 percent are undecided — so, there's a swing vote in play already.

I am going to call on Niall Ferguson to get us started.

NIALL FERGUSON: Thank you Rudyard, and thank you, ladies and gentlemen. I believe the 21st century will belong to China because most centuries have belonged to China. The 19th and 20th centuries were the exceptions. Eighteen of the last twenty centuries saw China as, by some margin, the largest economy in the world.

Let me begin with some demographics and economics: China is more of a continent than it is a country. A fifth of humanity lives there. It is forty times the size of Canada. If China were organized like Europe it would have to be divided up into ninety nation-states. Today there are eleven cities in China with a population of more than six million. There's only one city in Europe with a population of more than six million, and that's London. There are eleven European Union states with populations of less than six million. In thirty years China's economy has grown by a factor of very nearly ten, and

7

the International Monetary Fund (IMF) recently projected that it will be the largest economy in the world in five years' time. It's already taken over the United States as a manufacturer and as the world's biggest automobile market. And the demand for cars in China will increase by tenfold in the years to come. China will be using one fifth of all global energy by 2035. It used to be reliant on foreign direct investment, but today, with three trillion dollars of international reserves and a sovereign wealth fund of 200 billion dollars' worth of assets, China has become *the* investor.

What's perhaps most impressive is that China is catching up to other nations in terms of innovation and in terms of education. It's about to overtake Germany in terms regarding the number of new patents granted, and in a recent survey by the Organisation for Economic Co-operation and Development (OECD), the educational attainment of fifteen-year-old students in the region of Shanghai came top in mathematical attainment with a score of 600. The United States ranked twenty-fifth with a score of 487. You'll be glad to hear that Canada got a score of 527. That's better than the United States, but not good enough.

Ladies and gentlemen, it's not easy being a biographer debating against his own subject. It's a little bit as if James Boswell had to debate against Dr. Johnson. So, what I propose to do in a diplomatic way is to try to show to you that Dr. Kissinger and perhaps Fareed Zakaria are, through no fault of their own, on the wrong side of this debate. Let me quote from Dr. Kissinger's outstanding new book on the topic of China: "China's quest for equal partnership with the United States is no longer the outsized claim of a vulnerable country; it is increasingly the reality backed by financial and economic capacities." Or I could quote from Fareed Zakaria's excellent book *The Post-American World*: "China is a country whose scale dwarfs the United States. China is hungry for success."

It's fascinating that these two great geopolitical thinkers agree that China's economic challenge is also a challenge to the hegemony of the United States. Once again let me quote Dr. Kissinger: "An explicit American project to organize Asia on the basis of containing China or creating a bloc of democratic states for an ideological crusade is unlikely to succeed." He hopes, as he concludes in his book, for peaceful co-evolution. But he fears a repeat of what happened a hundred years ago when the rise of Germany challenged the predominance of the United Kingdom.

But it's not just about China for me. The key to China's dominance during the 21st century ultimately lies in the decline of the West. A financial crisis caused by excessive borrowing and subsidized gambling; a fiscal crisis that means the United States will soon be spending more on debt interest than on defence; a political crisis exemplified by a game of Russian roulette over the U.S. federal debt ceiling; and a moral crisis personified by a legislator named, implausibly, Weiner, sending miscellaneous women pictures of his naked torso. The 21st century will be China's because an overweight, over-leveraged, oversexed America, not to mention a dysfunctional Europe, are on the slide.

Four decades ago, President Richard Nixon understood this point sooner than most: "Well, you can just stop and think of what would happen if anybody with a decent system of government got control of that mainland. Good God, there'd be no power in the world that could even . . . I mean, you put 800 million Chinese to work under a decent system and they will be the leaders of the world." I salute the achievement of that administration in reopening Sino-American relations in 1972. No one contributed more to that achievement than Henry Kissinger. So I don't ask you to vote against him, but to vote in favour of his own analysis, which places him and his partner in this debate firmly on the pro side of the debate. I urge you to support the resolution.

RUDYARD GRIFFITHS: Fareed Zakaria, your opening statement, please.

FAREED ZAKARIA: Thank you very much. That's a hard act to follow. My role in this debate will be to lower the average age of this debating team, and I am going to try and do that as best I can without also lowering the average IQ, which I fear is also going to happen. So bear with me and Henry will correct all the mistakes I make — including, I hope, firing his biographer, which I think should be one of the first steps.

I was actually a little worried about having to debate with Henry because he is a legendary genius, but part of debating is listening to the other side, and I remember a story that was told to me about Henry. It is an example of what journalists call "too good to check," so I've never fact-checked it. The story goes like this: Henry Kissinger, as you know, has a legendary accent and friends of his who are German say, "He has an accent even in German." Apparently Henry Kissinger has an older brother who speaks American English without a German accent. So somebody asked his brother to explain the reason behind this difference. And he said, "It's very simple; Henry never listens."

I want to make three points about China. China is not going to be the dominant power during the 21st century. The century is not going to belong to China because of three factors: economic, political, and geopolitical. The first factor is economic — one thing we've realized over the course of the past decades is that nothing goes up in a straight line forever. China looks like it is about to inherit the world, but Japan looked like that for a while, too. It was the second largest economy in the world; I don't know how many of you remember all of the tales we were told about how the world was going to become Japanese. We were all going to be eating sushi — well, I guess we *are* all eating sushi — but the rest of that prediction didn't quite work out.

If you think about it, most Asian tigers have grown at a rate of about 9 percent a year for twenty to twenty-five years. And then they shift downward to a rate of 6 or 5 percent. I'm not predicting any kind of Chinese crash.

I am simply saying that China will follow that law of large numbers initially and then regress at some point to a slow growth rate, perhaps a little bit later than other nations because it is a much larger country.

It is also worth pointing out that there are massive inefficiencies built into the Chinese system. They have a huge property bubble. Their growth is highly inefficient. China's foreign direct investment each month is equal to India's yearly foreign direct investment, and still China grows only two percentage points faster than India. In other words, if you think about the quality of Chinese growth, it's not as impressive as it appears. It is massive investment, a huge number of airports, eight-lane highways, a high-speed rail that's being built, and if you look at what you are getting out of it in terms of the return on investment, it is not as impressive.

The UN recently published a report indicating that China is going to have a demographic collapse over the next twenty-five years. The population will decrease by 400 million people. There is no point in human history when a dominant power in the world was also declining demographically. It simply doesn't happen. And if you want to look at what a country in demographic decline looks like, look at Japan and ask yourself how powerful it is.

Even if China were the largest economy in the world, those numbers are based on something called "purchasing power parity." China's GDP becomes inflated because, for example, the cost of a haircut in Beijing is less than the cost of one in Toronto. But international power doesn't depend on the price of a haircut, it depends on foreign aid, oil, international investments, and aircraft carriers, and real, hard currency is required for all of those things, and that adjusts these numbers slightly.

Let's say that China does become the largest economy in the world. Does it have the political capacity to exercise the kind of leadership that is needed? Remember, Japan was the second largest economy in the world for decades, and I didn't see any kind of grand hegemonic design. Political capacity is required to be able to exercise that type of leadership. Henry's going to talk more about these issues, but I want to telegraph them by saying that China is a country ruled by a political system that is in crisis.

It is unclear whether or not the next succession that China goes through will look anything like the current one. China has not solved the basic problem of what it is going to do when it creates a middle class, and how the government will respond to the aspirations of those people. When Taiwan went through a similar process, there was a transition to democracy. When South Korea went through it, there was a transition to democracy. These transitions were not easy periods. They were fairly bloody and chaotic ones, and, as Niall has reminded us, China is a very large country and a very complex country. Imagine this kind of political instability and social instability in that process [China's transition].

Finally, I'll make one point about the geopolitics, and again, Henry will talk more about that. People like to talk about the rise of Asia. I grew up in India; there is no such thing as Asia. There's China, there's Japan, and there's India. They don't much like each other. And as China rises there is going to be a spirited response in India, in Japan, in Indonesia, in Vietnam, and in South Korea. We have already begun to see the stirrings of this. China is not rising in a vacuum. It is rising on a continent in which there are many, many competitors.

RUDYARD GRIFFITHS: David Li, you're next.

DAVID LI: Good evening, ladies and gentlemen. As the only debater from China I am extremely handicapped because we do not advocate debates in my culture, or in the educational system, especially not debates against an elderly sage. Today I would urge you to read each of the bestselling books written by my co-debaters. They are much better at explaining the huge amount of change in China over the past decades, as well as the mountain of challenges ahead, as Fareed has just explained to you. Buy their books — today, I am advocating their points.

I would like to share three simple points with you; they can be summarized by three keywords. The first keyword is energy. I would argue that the changes we have witnessed over the past decades in China are only halfway done at most. We are seeing continued change in China. Why? It is because there is energy. There's new energy in China's gas tank, energy for continued change, whether it's economic or political. Why? It is because the changes came from a spectacular clash of civilizations between China and the West as recently as 170 years ago.[1] The clash was a total failure for the Chinese. It was a big humiliation for us, and it has been remembered from generation to generation. Our children are still learning these lessons today.

And that humiliation created a huge reaction and over-reaction in Chinese society, in China's history, including the founding of the Chinese Communist Party ninety years ago. That was more about establishing a strong and independent China than spreading a proletariat revolution all over the world. So after the founding of the Republic, sixty-two years ago, we've seen overreaction from the Communist Party, and from the government, in the form of the Great Leap Forward, in the form of the Cultural Revolution — neither of which improved life for the Chinese, neither of which advanced the interests of the Chinese. That is, until thirty-three years ago, when bigger changes occurred, which we called Reform and Opening Up.

Reform implies gradual improvements in our institutions, whether they are political or economic. Opening Up refers to learning whatever is best in the West. Initially, people didn't believe in the message of reform and opening up, just as Fareed was saying. But our great leader Deng Xiaoping said, "No debates. Just do it." I guess Deng Xiaoping wouldn't be a fan of the Munk Debates. He would be a fan, perhaps, of Nike. Just do it. Indeed,

---

[1] Following the First Anglo–Chinese or Opium War, the Treaty of Nanking (1842) imposed a number of obligations on China, including the formal cession of Hong Kong to Britain. The financial and trade-related concessions imposed by this treaty, and by other "unequal treaties" with foreign powers, were keenly felt as a humiliation by China.

the last thirty years of change have demonstrated the power of reform and opening up. Young people today are not satisfied with the progress we have made. They are eager to push for more reform, more opening up, using the power of the Internet. So, that is the first message — energy. The energy is still there, in the gas tank.

But where are we driving to? What's the destination? The destination relates to the second keyword, revival. The destination is the revival of that great civilization from 1,500 years ago, the Tang Dynasty. Revival is not revenge against the West, or to emulate the success of the United States in the absolute dominance of the world. Rather, it is the revival of a peaceful, self-confident, open-minded civilization such as the Tang Dynasty. That is the destination of this change, which is at most halfway through.

The third keyword I would like to share with you is influence. What kind of influence will China have in the world ninety years from now? I would like to argue that the influence will be multi-dimensional. First, China's emergence has given hope to those who live in the poor regions of the world, such as Africa and other under-developed regions. The people who live in these regions say to themselves, "China has been poor. China has been constrained in natural resources. If China can make it, surely we can as well." So we are giving hope to many of the world's poor. That's the first dimension.

The second dimension of influence is that China's emergence gives us an alternative model for social and economic institutions; different from those in the West, different from those in the United States. In this model — compared with the United States and other Western models — more weight is given to social welfare, to social well-being, to social stability, rather than to pure individual liberty.

The third dimension of influence is international relations. China's revival of great civilizations such as the Tang Dynasty gives us a new focus on international relations in which China is looking for peace and collaboration. We saw this over the past two and a half years during the global financial crisis.

So overall I won't impose my conclusion upon you. I would like to ask you to draw your own conclusions: continuous change with energy, revival of a great civilization, and a positive international influence. You draw your own conclusions. Thank you.

RUDYARD GRIFFITHS: Dr. Kissinger.

HENRY KISSINGER: For somebody who was brought up speaking German, six minutes are barely enough to speak a word. My colleagues have spoken about the magnitude of China. I respect its tremendous achievement. And nobody would deny — in fact, I would affirm — what China has achieved in the forty years that I have been able to observe it directly. But the issue before us is whether or not the 21st century belongs to China. I would say that China will be preoccupied with enormous problems domestically, and preoccupied with its immediate environment, during the 21st century. And because of this I have enormous difficulty imagining a world dominated by China. Indeed, as I will conclude, I believe that the concept that any one country will dominate the world is, in itself, a misunderstanding of the world in which we now live.

China has achieved great things economically, but as a country it has to produce 24 million jobs every year; it has to absorb 6 million people moving into the cities every year; it has to deal with a floating population of 150 to 200 million. It has to accommodate a society in which the coastal regions are at the level of advanced countries while the interior regions are at the level of underdevelopment. And it has to accommodate all of this in a political system that must take care of both economic change and political adaptation that will inevitably result from the huge figures involved in the economic change.

From a geopolitical perspective, China has historically been surrounded by a group of smaller countries which were not individually able to threaten China, but which, united, could pose a threat to China. Therefore, historically, Chinese foreign policy can be described as barbarian management. China has never had to deal with a world of countries of approximately equal strength. So to adjust to such a world is in itself a profound challenge to China, which now has fourteen countries on its borders, some of which are small but can project their nationality into China, some of which are large and historically significant, so that any attempt by China to dominate the world would evoke a counter-reaction that would be disastrous for the peace of the world.

As for the quote that Niall Ferguson — who, of course, is my biographer, so he will have the last word no matter what I say — used about the military containment of China, I would say that one of our challenges is to accommodate the rights of China. One of China's challenges is to accommodate itself to a world in which it is not hegemonial as it has been for eighteen of the last twenty centuries.

So if I may take the liberty of restating the motion before us: the issue before the world is not whether the 21st century belongs to China. The issue before the world is whether or not during the 21st century, as China undoubtedly gets stronger, we in the West can work with China. And the issue is also whether China can work with us to create an international structure in which, perhaps for the first time in history, a rising state has been incorporated into an international system and strengthened peace and progress. In my book, I say that, based on my experience, the prospects are not optimistic. But, on the other hand, we have never had to deal with proliferation, environment, cyberspace, and a whole set of other problems that can be dealt with only on a universal basis.

My conclusion is that the issue is not whether the 21st century belongs to China, but whether we can make China belong to a more universal conception in the 21st century.

RUDYARD GRIFFITHS: A fascinating series of arguments have begun to crystallize in this debate, and to keep it going I want to ask both teams of debaters to quickly respond to what they've heard during their opponents' opening statements. Specifically, I'd like them to address what they disagree with most. Niall, as we agreed, I want to come to you first for your rebuttal.

NIALL FERGUSON: My question to Fareed is, if you're right and China is going to repeat Japanese history, just think what that means considering Japan's much smaller size and considering China's relatively low level of development, as both of you have pointed out. If you're right and China is going to re-enact Japan's economic history, then it surely will own the 21st century. Because before it slows down in the way that Japan has since the late 1980s, it will achieve an enormous share not only of global GDP but also of global power, because unlike Japan, China never lost its sovereignty through the kind of military defeat that Japan suffered in 1945. So both economically and geopolitically, the prospect of China repeating Japanese history should really be quite a scary one for your side of the debate.

RUDYARD GRIFFITHS: Fareed?

FAREED ZAKARIA: The Japanese example simply illustrates that nothing moves in a straight line. Countries, particularly as they ascend the economic modernization scale, find that they have problems. If you look at the number of countries that have been able to get past about $12,000 per capita GDP over the last 100 years, it is an astonishingly small number. It is about five.

There are a lot of countries that manage to do well — with basic manufacturing, the beginnings of the reform process, the government getting out of the way of the economy. Then it turns out that every element of the society has to be modernized to move up into the top tier that South Korea, Taiwan, Singapore, and Hong Kong have been able to reach. I would like to point out simply that China — with the economic, demographic, political, and geopolitical problems it faces — might find that that last period of economic ascent will be somewhat rocky and complex. As Henry pointed out, it may require China to stay internally focused and absorbed in a way that will not allow it to project enormous hegemonic power.

I don't doubt that China is going to have an enormous economy. I don't doubt that China is going to be an enormous player on the world stage. The question is, will it *own* the 21st century, will it dominate? And I say for all those reasons it's not going to do that.

RUDYARD GRIFFITHS: David, come back to the Japanese example; it was a subject of a lot of debate. The years of GDP growth, the close state co-ordination of their economy, and more than that the sense in the 1980s that Japan was a lot like China — a society with a lot of homogeneity, a lot of energy. Why isn't Japan's recent past China's near future?

DAVID LI: Let me respond to your question, and to Fareed's points, and to Dr. Kissinger's points altogether. Your arguments are correct. These points are even stronger if we are talking about China twenty or even thirty years ago. Despite all these claims, China has been growing. China has been changing for the past thirty years. And my point is that today's China, despite all the mounting challenges, is still changing.

Let's compare China and Japan. I don't think that there had been any fundamental changes in Japan before the collapse starting in the early 1990s. In China we do see fundamental changes. Also, Japan has been learning from China. I would not argue that Japan was one of the primary cultures in the world where China is concerned, at least until the spectacular financial crash took place in Western countries.

On Fareed's point about the economic growth rate, I fully agree that an economy as large as China's can never have double digit GDP growth indefinitely. It will slow down. But when the United States was emerging, it wasn't growing nearly as fast as China is currently. The United States slowed down significantly, long before it became the world's dominant power. And yet it kept growing. In today's China, I see energy, I see ongoing changes.

Finally, I would like to address one of Dr. Kissinger's points. He has been referring back to the past eighteen centuries in China. I completely agree with him, but there is one difference. In today's China, we have been sending a huge number of young kids to study abroad. How many? Imagine six times the size of the student population at the University of Toronto, that's the number of Chinese students studying in the United States and in Canada. These are sources of change. These kids are learning. So I do think China's emergence will be different from that of the United States, and I also think it will not face the same problems as Japan faced.

RUDYARD GRIFFITHS: Dr. Kissinger, would you like to offer a rebuttal?

HENRY KISSINGER: That China is changing — that is undoubtedly the case. If one compares what China looked like in 1971 to what it looks like today, it has changed physically and it has changed demographically in a fundamental way through the one child per family policy. The latter has also, in a way, changed the values in China. In about thirty years, there will be only about two people who are of working age for every person of retirement age. In 2005, there were 9.2 people that were able to take care of retirement-age people, so this creates a different set of attitudes.

But one must not confuse magnitude with global influence. China will have to be preoccupied with the adjustments to urbanization, with the adjustments to demography, and with the adjustments to an international system in which it will be a permanent participant rather than the centre of the universe, as it has historically conceived of itself. These are soluble problems, but they should not be compared to Western notions of imperialism.

Historically, China's role internationally has been based on gaining respect for its conduct. It has not been geared culturally for a global role. I believe that for

China to manage its environment and its domestic situation, co-operation with the West — rather than attempts to dominate the West — will be required.

RUDYARD GRIFFITHS: Fareed, would you like to weigh in on this point also?

FAREED ZAKARIA: I want to ask Niall a question. I suppose I could have read all of Niall's forty-six books to find quotations that contradict his current position, but instead I'm going to put this very simply. Niall is a very keen student of geopolitics, and I wondered what he made of the fact that China is rising — and it is undoubtedly rising — but not in a geopolitical vacuum. If you consider the past year, China had a good year. It had a financial crisis and it came out of it feeling confident. And consider China's behaviour. In Copenhagen, China humiliated the United States and humiliated the president of the United States, and refused to sign up for a deal. It angered Japan enormously with its position on the issue of the Senkaku Islands.[2] When the North Koreans sank a South Korean boat, and the South Koreans asked the Chinese to condemn the action, they refused, which enraged the

[2] A group of uninhabited islands in the East China Sea, located between Okinawa, Japan, and the island of Taiwan. The islands (known as the Diaoyu Islands in China) had been under Chinese sovereignty for several centuries, but controlled by Japan from 1895 until the end of the Second World War. The United States then administered the islands until 1972, when they reverted back to Japan under the terms of a U.S.-Japanese treaty. Since the early 1970s, however, sovereignty of the islands has been claimed by both the People's Republic of China and the Republic of China (Taiwan).

South Koreans. The Vietnamese and Filipinos were also enraged because China asserted sovereignty over the South China Sea. That's just in one year! And those instances occurred when China hadn't even gotten to the point where it is considered the dominant economic power in the world.

Do you think that all these countries are going to simply accept Chinese domination? Or are we likely to see a spirited response from the Indias, Vietnams, South Koreas, Japans, and Indonesias of the world? All of a sudden this proposition of a dominant China doesn't look as rosy as it did.

NIALL FERGUSON: Thanks, Fareed, for that question. I've noticed in your recent columns in *Time* magazine you've been dabbling in economics. So this gives me an opportunity to help you out. The thing about China's growth during the financial crisis is that it fundamentally altered China's role in the world economy. Up until the financial crisis the main story was that China was competing with other emerging markets for market share in developed economies like Canada's or the United States'. China was an exporter of cheap goods, and essentially it was able to beat out most of its emerging market competitors with the so-called "China price." And then the financial crisis struck and those developed economies went into recession or near depression.

What happened? China engaged in the biggest and most successful stimulus in the world, and in so doing, its role changed. It ceased to be a competitor with other emerging markets, and it became their market of first resort. They found that the most dynamic market they could sell to was China's. And so, in an amazing reversal of fortune, trade patterns around the world shifted, and China's Asian neighbours — including India, where you were born — discovered a new China that was not a competitor, but a market to which they could sell.

That trend is going to continue because the whole aim of China's latest five-year plan is to shift from exports to domestic demand to consumption. That's why the idea that all these Asian countries are going to band together against nasty China is a total fantasy. They depend on China economically more now than they ever have. And if you go to Seoul and talk to people there, or if you talk to Mukesh Ambani, India's richest man, he'll tell you just how big China's business is for the rest of Asia now. And that seems to me to be a very good reason why the 21st century is going to belong to China, because all of those Asian markets are going to belong to China.

RUDYARD GRIFFITHS: I'm going to go to you, David, and then back to Fareed, and finish with Dr. Kissinger before we take a couple of questions from the audience.

DAVID LI: Fareed was absolutely right in observing the tensions during the past year. But we have to go deeper. We don't have to stay on the surface, as they do on television. I'm sorry, television is important, especially Fareed's program, which I like very much. But we have to go beyond the surface. Who are the aggressors? Who were the provocative parties? It was never China.

For example, take the issue of the Senkaku Islands and Japan's involvement. The Japanese government arrested and used domestic law against Chinese sailors. The Chinese side was trying to make peace. Consider the Copenhagen negotiations — China was trying to come to a meaningful agreement with other countries. The Chinese side is extremely handicapped because whatever the Chinese government promises today, the Chinese government has to honour in the future, because we cannot claim we have changed our parliament and that the new parliament has nullified the agreement.

In the case of negotiations with the United States, it was a show for the new president, Barack Obama. The president was trying to negotiate, but the deal would have been killed by Congress. That tactic would never work in China. I would suggest you look at other evidence. For almost three years during the financial crisis, China was trying to stabilize the global financial system. Unlike many other currencies, the renminbi (RMB)[3] did not depreciate against the U.S. dollar during the peak days of the crisis.

Also, China did not sell massive amounts of Treasury bond holdings during the financial crisis. China has been the most patient long-term investor supporting today's Europe and supporting the U.S. government today. So I suggest looking at the big picture.

---

[3]   The "people's currency" and official currency of the People's Republic of China, introduced in 1949. The primary unit of the renminbi is the yuan.

FAREED ZAKARIA: Niall is, of course, an incredibly accomplished economic historian, and he understands the economics of Asia. But I would point out that throughout history people have gone to war and countries have had spirited geopolitical rivalries despite the fact that they have been economically interdependent.

The first great historian, Thucydides, talked about the Peloponnesian War, and his first explanation for the reason that war occurred was honour and dignity. That war had nothing to do with economics. Look at Europe on the eve of the First World War — it was a continent that was economically more interdependent by some measures than the countries of the world today. The level of economic interdependence between Britain and Germany at that time was such that it was in some ways madness that these two countries went to war, but still they did. There was a very famous book written by a young historian who talked about the fact that perhaps Britain should not have gone to war, because that was insanity. That book was called *The Pity of War*. Oh, wait a minute! That historian was Niall Ferguson.

NIALL FERGUSON: So you've read one of my books, then.

RUDYARD GRIFFITHS: Before we end the rebuttal part of this debate, I'd like to allow Dr. Kissinger to have the last word.

HENRY KISSINGER: I think it's three to one against my friend Niall. Our Chinese friend is saying that China has suffered a great deal, has been provoked during a century of Western exploitation, and that it's not trying to dominate the world. As I understand it, he is saying this: when the West wants to discuss climate or the financial system, our tendency is to say that China can be a stakeholder, it can be a participant in a system that they did not participate in creating. So the issue is whether or not it is possible to create an international system with China as a participant without dominating it. This is really what we are debating.

If I understand the observations of our Chinese colleague, he's not saying that China will dominate the world. He's saying that China is making great progress and that China wants to be heard, and that the United States should not present them with a finished product and ask for their agreement on such issues as climate change. All of this we agree upon, on this side of the aisle. So, David, if you would like to move your chair over to our side, we will welcome you.

RUDYARD GRIFFITHS: We're going to move into the question and answer portion of the debate now. We're going to break it down into the following subjects. The subjects are economic, political and cultural, and of course geopolitical. To begin with the section on the economy, I want to go to someone in the audience who's written a number of best-selling books on economic themes, including *Dead Aid: Why Aid Is Not Working and How There Is a Better Way for Africa*, a bestseller in Canada, and *How the West Was Lost: Fifty Years of Economic*

Folly — and the Stark Choices Ahead, and she is Dambisa Moyo.

DAMBISA MOYO: My question is for Mr. Li and Mr. Ferguson. Until now, a key piece of China's development strategy has been to use soft power, vast resources, to accumulate and access natural resources such as land, water, energy, and minerals. And effectively, China's been freeloading off the United States, which has been underwriting public goods such as national security around the world. As we head toward a world population of nine billion people in 2050, and add two billion into the middle class in 2030, my question to you is, how aggressive do you think China will become in her efforts to secure natural resources? In other words, what is the likelihood that China moves from the soft power strategy of accumulating resources to one where she depends more aggressively on hard power and, therefore, adopts more military and colonial-like strategies of accumulating resources, particularly in the context of Africa?

NIALL FERGUSON: Dambisa, it's great to have you here, and I hesitate to answer a question from you on the subject of Africa. But it seems to me, having recently visited Zambia and having been to Senegal and Namibia last year, that something very important is happening in sub-Saharan Africa. China is leading a whole new developmental push, which is radically different in its nature from the aid programs you persuasively argued had been a failure when the West tried them. This is a developmental strategy based on self-interest. China is developing natural resources such as copper in the Zambian copper belt because it desperately needs copper to wire its vast new cities. But the effect in Africa is by no means all bad, and I think it's a really big misrepresentation to suggest that this is a rerun of 19th-century colonialism. That wasn't the question in my mind when I went to Zambia. It wasn't the answer that I found.

That wasn't the Chinese approach, and in many ways I think what they are doing is in line with what you argued in *Dead Aid*. The Chinese are investing. They're trying to make money. They're letting the market drive African economic development rather than handouts and a culture of dependency. Would this ultimately lead to conflict of the sort that you suggest, a sort of scramble for Africa, as it did in the late 19th century? It's conceivable, but I see absolutely no sign of it at the moment. There's only one country scrambling for Africa right now, and that country is China.

DAVID LI: Let me follow Niall's great points by adding three simple observations. The first observation has to do with intention. China doesn't have the intention of repeating the colonialism of previous centuries. On the contrary, China has been working hard to collaborate with African countries. Consider the African Union Summit, which took place about three years ago. Most African leaders and business people were very enthusiastic about Chinese investments there.

The second observation relates to capacity. Consider the Chinese reality. We are still an extremely poor economy — the GDP per capita is around 4,000 U.S. dollars — so there's a long way to go for economic growth. Meanwhile, that implies that there is absolutely no capacity to colonize all of the African countries, even if China wanted to do so.

My third observation is more generally about China itself. Within China there have been tremendous efforts to push for new technologies to conserve resources, new technologies to promote energy efficiency, and new policies to encourage conservation. So I think it is clear that China is trying to develop a new pattern of modernization that will give hope to those in the world's poor nations.

RUDYARD GRIFFITHS: I want to ask you, Dr. Kissinger, isn't this one of the traps that nations that begin to assume global power fall into? Do you think China is at risk of reaching beyond itself to defend these resources?

HENRY KISSINGER: That China will want to acquire resources for its industry is a natural evolution. Whether it believes that in order to have the access to its resources it must also be militarily dominant, that's another decision. If you consider Germany before World War I, the world would probably have been able to live with the idea that Germany had the largest land army. But when it tried to develop the world's largest naval force on top of that, it began to threaten the long-term existence of Great Britain. So there were two challenges.

We have to understand that China will get stronger, and that we cannot react neurologically to every indication of Chinese strength. But China has to learn some self-limitation in the way it vindicates its interests around the world. Both of these ideas have to exist and cannot be done by one nation alone. It has to be done collaboratively.

FAREED ZAKARIA: Can I add just one comment, which is I think that David said that China's investments in Africa are very popular; I think it would be more accurate to say that China's investments in Africa are very popular with [Africa's] dictators. I was in Kenya a year ago and I asked a group of Kenyan parliamentarians what their main concern was — we were talking about democracy and human rights — and they said the single biggest concern they have is that China is going around Africa's governments to make deals with Africa's dictators, and there are no questions asked and there is no accountability on any human rights issues. I would argue that that is possibly an exaggeration, but certainly something they have to be worried about in a long-term geopolitical sense. We thought we had very stable relations with many of the countries in the Middle East; it turns out we had very stable relations with all of the dictators in the Middle East.

NIALL FERGUSON: Hang on a second, Fareed. I'm an historian more than I am an economist. Remind me, are you saying that Western powers never did deals with

Western dictators, and that this is some new and terrible deformity of Chinese policy? I go to Africa, too, and I spoke to the miners in the copper belt who had no jobs when the state-owned mining system collapsed and have jobs now because the Chinese reopened the mines. And they not only reopened them but extended them. It's not fair to say that China only deals with African dictators. It deals with African democracies. It deals with the governments it finds in Africa, including the governments that Western powers have propped up for too many years.

FAREED ZAKARIA: I make no apologies for the West on this issue. I'm simply pointing out that China is doing what it is doing with the leadership class, and that that leadership may not reflect the wishes of the entire African public.

NIALL FERGUSON: Would you say that Africa would be better off if China didn't invest there?

FAREED ZAKARIA: I'm not saying that at all.

NIALL FERGUSON: Would Africa be better off if China weren't its biggest trading partner? I think that's the kind of hypocritical argument that I'd find quite annoying if I were Chinese.

FAREED ZAKARIA: You're obviously finding it annoying even though you are not Chinese.

RUDYARD GRIFFITHS: Staying on the theme of economics, I'm holding in my hand what many people consider to be the quintessential consumer success product of the last decade, the Apple iPhone. This phone is manufactured in China. It is however, designed in California. The software that powers it was conceived by Steve Jobs and his team at Apple. And that wow factor that makes this such a coveted device leads me to ask both Niall and David, can China innovate in the same way, on the same scale as Apple, as Google, or as RIM has here in Canada? Because they've got to do it if you think that they can own the 21st century.

DAVID LI: The answer is, yes, they can. Remember, no very poor country could innovate overnight. It's a learning process. As I said before, it's about opening up, learning what works in the West, sending hundreds of thousands of students to the West to learn and then gradually innovate. Nearly thirty years ago, China couldn't innovate. Now we have rapid trans-railroads while the United States is still struggling. Today we have cars which are not only cheaper but also more efficient than those built by General Motors. Remember, most of GM's profit comes from China today. If it were not for Chinese operations, GM would have used more U.S. government money for its bailout. It's a simple fact.

I'm sure China will innovate in the long run. It's a gradual learning process. But whether or not China will have an iPhone in the future is a different issue. It's a different level of innovation — iPhones and iPads could only be invented in the United States. China has different economic and social institutions; it will not be on the cutting edge of innovation. But you don't need to be on the cutting edge of innovation in order to be a respected and important country in the world.

NIALL FERGUSON: You know, I've heard that story about the iPhone so many times, and it's a symptom of Western complacency. As if we'll always have the cool ideas and they'll always do the assembly line. That idea is ten years out of date. We're not talking about the future here. China is going to overtake Germany in terms of internationally recognized patents in the next couple of years, and that is because of a huge effort on the part of China's educational institutions, like the one where David works, to raise the game in research and development, in producing people with Ph.D.'s. And I'm not talking about Ph.D.'s in media studies, but Ph.D.'s in engineering and in physics.

RUDYARD GRIFFITHS: Fareed, I'd like to come to you on this point as well. Can China innovate without a free and open society?

FAREED ZAKARIA: First, let me say that I agree with Niall and David on this issue. It is a mistake to believe that there is some sort of genetic deformation that doesn't allow the Chinese to innovate. Of course they're going to innovate, of course they're going to do things that are interesting. The point that Henry and I keep making is, they're going to innovate, we're going to innovate, this is going to be a world of multiplicities. That's why I didn't call my book *The Chinese World* or *The Indian World*. It is genuinely a post-American world. There will be a lot of innovation.

But I do have one qualifying thought: if you look at Apple and think about what constitutes innovation, Apple is generally regarded as the most innovative company in the world right now. It tops all the lists. Apple spends as much money on research and development in one decade as Microsoft spends in one year. If you look at the lists of research and development spending, Apple is ranked 82nd. It spends 50 percent of what most computer companies spend. Apple's innovations are designed with the ways human beings use technology in mind. That may be something you learn when you get a Ph.D. in media studies.

And by the way, this is true throughout history. With the invention of the sewing machine, Singer's great skill was not coming up with the best machine. It was that he figured out that he could sell it to women on an instalment plan. Nobody had ever sold machinery to women before. Google's great innovation may not actually be the search engine. It may be the advertising program that goes along with it. So part of what innovation is, is this strange combination of science and consumer behaviour. I mean the great invention that launched capitalism was double-entry bookkeeping. It wasn't some scientific gizmo.

Of course, China will innovate in its own way, but there is something about the ecosystem of America that has all of the things that we all know. Also, I think most importantly, Americans have the ability to question hierarchy, which is absolutely key. I hear people talking about Asian education and the Tiger Mom style of parenting.[4] You know, I went through an Asian education system. I think it's pretty lousy. It's rote memorization toward some big exam, and when you've taken the exam you promptly forget everything you've learned.

The American system is much better in that it teaches students to think, it teaches students to problem-solve, it teaches students to love learning for the rest of their lives, it is a continuous process, and it doesn't make anyone feel ashamed of failure. The ability to fail efficiently is an incredibly powerful part of innovation. So China will innovate, but I think that is something very special about the United States.

RUDYARD GRIFFITHS: I want to move on to the second part of the question and answer session, which is politics and culture. To kick us off, I'd like to call on Janice Stein, the head of the Munk School of Global Affairs.

JANICE STEIN: This question is for David Li and Fareed Zakaria. The world watched recently with astonishment as young people streamed into the squares in Tunisia and in Egypt to demand political rights, and to demand that authoritarian and corrupt leaders leave the scene. Now, the parallels between the Arab world and China

---

[4]   A reference to *Battle Hymn of the Tiger Mother* (2011), law professor Amy Chua's account of her attempts to raise her two daughters in the traditional, strict Chinese manner.

are far from perfect. China is a mature society, the Arab world is young. China has created hundreds of millions of jobs, Arab governments have not. But China, like the Arab world, tolerates almost no dissent, and again, like the Arab world, there is growing income inequality within China. So my question is, as China is about to undergo a leadership transition,[5] will there be growing demand for political rights in China, and how will the leadership cope?

DAVID LI: Thank you for asking this question. I knew it would come up. I don't need to be reminded of the Arab Spring — we knew it would happen from day one. After economic success, people in China knew that there would be more voices, there would be more demand for the right to express opinions and political participation in decision-making.

From day one, people in China knew that economic institutional change would go hand in hand with political institutional change. I think the biggest misunderstanding about China is the idea that we don't have political institutional change. We do, starting with the way leaders are being selected. Today, the way leaders are being selected and the way public decisions are being made is much, much more sophisticated than it was before. Young people in China are able to express their opinions on the Internet, and in most cases their voices are being heard and public decisions are being changed.

---

[5] China's leadership is set to change in 2012 with the election of a new president and successor to Hu Jintao.

39

So I would invite you all to go to China, to talk to young people, to visit Chinese web sites, to understand the new method reform, to understand the new ways in which people express their opinions and express their dissidence. And you will also see a new way in which public decision-makers are taking into account the opinions of people, especially young people.

FAREED ZAKARIA: I would have agreed with David five years ago. It was very clear that there was a movement toward very gradual and very limited, but also very real, political reform. I think that over the last five years we have seen that economic reform and economic growth have proceeded apace, but there has been a drawing back of any kind of political reform. And with events around the world such as the Arab Spring, this makes it more difficult for China to maintain political control. What we don't see in China is a willingness to open up, and an attempt to announce a series of ambitious political reforms. In fact, there is a closing down. If you type the word "jasmine" into Google in China you will come up against a blank page, because of a fear that somehow the Jasmine Revolution[6] will take root in China. If you look at the Internet in general, China has, by some accounts, a million people monitoring the Internet. Text phone messages are also monitored.

---

[6]   The popular uprising in Tunisia that started in December 2010 and led to the ouster of president Zine El Abidine Ben Ali in January 2011. Tunisian journalist and blogger Zied El Hani has taken credit for the phrase, a reference to the country's national flower.

I can tell you about my one, personal slice of this. I got an interview with Wen Jiabao for my program, and it was a very important interview that I was honoured to get. The Chinese government announced that it was taking place because it was seen as very important. Premier Wen made some fairly harmless comments about how China would eventually evolve politically. The interview was banned on Chinese TV, it was taken off Chinese web sites. Then a group of Chinese journalists protested the fact that the interview had been censored, and their protest letter was promptly taken off of their web site. This does not strike me as political reform. This strikes me as a kind of circling of the wagons, a fear of what might happen next. Clearly China has been giving greater and greater freedom to its people. I don't doubt that at all. But they have to figure out how they are going to create a political system that accommodates this rising middle class in a world where people are demanding greater and greater accountability from their leaders.

When I compare India and China I think to myself, China has solved all the small problems. They've built the best roads and the best highways and the best high-speed rail, and they've done this so magnificently that it puts India to shame. But India has solved one big problem, which is what it will look like twenty-five years from now politically. It will be the same crazy, chaotic democracy it is today. What will China be twenty-five years from now, politically? Will there still be a mandarin elite? The Communist Party of China is the most elite political organization in the world today.

Everybody looks like David, they all have Ph.D.'s and they're engineers, but that's not China. The people they rule are this vast mass of peasantry, and those people are not reflected in the political system. Their views, to a large extent, are filtered through many mechanisms. That strikes me as a huge political challenge for China going forward.

RUDYARD GRIFFITHS: Dr. Kissinger, I think the audience wants to hear you on this question, too.

HENRY KISSINGER: I believe that the next decade will see China wrestling with the problem of how it will bring its political institutions in line with its economic development. When there are vast economic changes, the migration of people, the spread of education, it is absolutely inevitable that that question will be one of the dominant issues of the new leadership, and that question is coming up in a year and a half. Whatever form it will take, whether it will be in the form of Western parliamentary democracy or some new form that we haven't seen yet, the outcome will have to include more transparency and more participation. And I believe the next leadership change will reflect this. This is also why I do not believe that a country that will be so preoccupied with fundamental change will also have time to concentrate on dominating the world.

RUDYARD GRIFFITHS: I'm going to let Niall respond.

NIALL FERGUSON: I remember reading a book a few years back with a title like *The Future of Freedom* in which a brilliant young journalist argued that there were problems with Western democracy, and especially with American democracy, that were only going to get worse. Hey, that was you, Fareed!

I know that Dr. Kissinger will agree with me on this, though he doesn't need to move over to the pro side yet — we are making a big mistake if we think there is one universal model of Western democracy that absolutely everybody is going to adopt at some point between now and 2050. If you think that that is what the future of the world is going to look like, you are going to be one very, very disappointed person. Starting in the Middle East, the chances of Western-style democracy emerging in any of these countries has to be between 0 and 5 percent at best. David raised the possibility of alternative models for democracy at the beginning of his thoughtful opening remarks. And I want you to think very seriously about what that implies. Singapore's government is not worried about a Jasmine Revolution. Singapore is the model. Think of China as a giant, technocratic Singapore, in which the one-party state evolves itself to avoid the catastrophe, or a collapse similar to that of the Soviet experience.

My second point, and this is where Dr. Kissinger and I differ, is that it is precisely when nations are struggling with internal political problems and challenges from below that they are most likely to pursue a more assertive and aggressive foreign policy. This must be one of the lessons of modern history, indeed of ancient history. And that is one of the reasons why I think it is precisely at this time of political stress that we are likely to see a more nationalistic and a more assertive China. That is one of the reasons I'm arguing for this motion.

RUDYARD GRIFFITHS: To start off our final portion of this question and answer period, I want to call on someone who's thought long and hard about the practicalities of China's rise. He's the former U.S. secretary of defence, William Cohen.

WILLIAM COHEN: If I could, I'd like to respond to Mr. Ferguson's comments in reference to Singapore. I was there a couple of weeks ago for the so-called Shangri-La Dialogues.[7] Secretary [Robert] Gates was there, and he made a very strong statement about the need for the United States to remain deeply engaged in the Asia-Pacific region. And he made the statement to satisfy the Asian nations, many of which are anxious about China. One young man I talked to — you quoted him in your book, Fareed — said that no one in Asia wants to be dominated by China. There is no aspiration for the Chinese dream, as there might be for the American dream. But there is a growing concern that as China continues to expand its economy it is also expanding its military. And there is a concern that the United States perhaps is looking inwardly now

[7] The International Institute for Strategic Studies (IISS) Asia Security Summit; named for the Shangri-La Hotel in Singapore, where meetings have been held since the forum's inception in 2002.

because of our debt problems, and that we will not be there in sufficient numbers. So they would like for the United States to become even more engaged.

Fareed, you said in your book that the United States must look for ways to co-operate with China. And there are a number of things that we can always co-operate on, and the list is pretty public. But there are also areas of friction, be it Taiwan, or the South China Sea. And you suggest that we need to draw lines. Now, we can't draw them everywhere, but the matter of the South China Sea does raise questions in terms of Indonesia, Malaysia, the Philippines, and other nations in the region. Most ironically, Vietnam is asking the United States to play a role in helping to solve the issues of sovereignty and territorial integrity. So the question I have for you or Dr. Kissinger is, would you suggest or support drawing the line at China's assertion of sovereignty over the South China Sea?

HENRY KISSINGER: To answer your specific question, I think freedom of the seas is a fundamental principle of American policy, and it has been a fundamental principle of the international system. So I would oppose the notion that any sea should be treated as a territorial issue. Next, there are a series of specific issues about the possession of a group of islands and rocks, and that should be dealt with through negotiation. But on this fundamental issue, I would apply the principle of freedom of the seas to the South China Sea, as I would to any other open ocean. The second point I want to make, however, is this: while we can define the emerging relationship with China as an ability to draw lines, I believe it would be extraordinarily dangerous to begin thinking of international relations as a question of the military containment of China. It is not a question of military containment. It is a question of dealing with China's inevitable rise. China has to restrain itself, within definable limits.

The United States cannot ask China to solve all of our internal problems for us. We have to remain competitive. If we remain competitive, then the next challenge is to see whether a dialogue can develop between China and the United States, and other countries that share the same view on what we intend the world to look like five to ten years from now. I keep asking the question that Niall asked in his first book, which is this: if the leaders of Europe had known in 1914 what the world would look like in 1990, would they have believed that what happened in Sarajevo[8] justified the tens of millions of casualties that resulted? Similarly, I believe the leaders of the world now have to ask themselves, and the leaders of China have to ask themselves, how the evolution should be managed in a way that is co-operative rather than confrontational. I conducted foreign policy on balance of power principles. I know how to play that game. So it's not that I wouldn't know how the United States should play it.

I once spoke to a Chinese group, and somebody got

---

[8] The assassination of Archduke Franz Ferdinand of Austria and his wife, Sophie, in Sarajevo on June 28, 1914 — an event which led to the outbreak of the First World War.

up and said, "You're a great friend of China, but we also read your books. And in your books you talk about the balance of power. How are you going to manage the balance of power?" And I said, "Look around. Look at the countries that border China. Ask yourself whether or not this is a problem that is conceivable." What I'm suggesting is that the South China Sea is a clear case: it should not be claimed by any nation.

But what we really have to ask is that the top leaders begin to ask some of the same questions that have been asked during this debate — to look at where we want to be five to ten years from now and work back from that, rather than deal with crisis management month by month and be in a situation when every time the leaders meet there is a terrific communiqué, and then two months later someone is asking, "Where did the Chinese go wrong, where did the West go wrong?" That is my fundamental view, so on the South China Sea it's clear where we should come out with respect to freedom of navigation. But that's just a symptom. What is required is an understanding that we are heading into a new world order with universal issues, and that this world order cannot be organized using the same principles as our customary, conventional thinking. And this is when the relationship with China will become important, because China is rising. The question is, can China learn restraint? And can the United States learn to accommodate a reduction of our previous influence? It is that with which we need to deal.

RUDYARD GRIFFITHS: Fareed, can America learn a pattern of restraint in this new phase? Give us your sense of where the American polity is at vis-à-vis China. Are they willing to accommodate its rise?

FAREED ZAKARIA: Everybody tends to view the United States as having this vacillating foreign policy — that it's unable to get its act together and the policy is constantly shifting. And on China, I have to say that I think that the opposite is the case. Since Henry Kissinger opened China to the world, and opened U.S. relations with China, the United States has had a remarkably consistent policy toward China. That policy has been to integrate China into the world, to help China gain the knowledge, the know-how, the technology, the capital, and the institutional frameworks that will help it become a productive, thriving member of the international community. We have followed that under Democratic presidents and under Republican presidents. We have maintained an extraordinary consistency of policy, even on issues such as red lines, such as our relationship with Taiwan, and our relationship with the Dalai Lama. Every president has maintained a very strong, co-operative relationship with China while also maintaining some core interests and values that were important for the United States.

My greatest worry about U.S.-Chinese relations right now isn't the United States. I think the United States will continue to play the same role, and has been trying to do so. The United States has been willing to reform the International Monetary Fund (IMF) and the World

Bank, and all the international institutions, to properly reflect the rise of China and other emerging market countries. Let's be honest, the countries that haven't wanted to do it are the Europeans, because their voting will be diluted in this process.

The greater danger is that as China undergoes the kind of political transformation that Henry has been talking about, it might find itself on a very different road. And here I'm quoting Niall Ferguson, who has said, quite rightly, China is becoming more nationalistic, more assertive, and more arrogant. There is a growing sense in China that the policies that Deng Xiaoping outlined — hide your light under a bushel, co-operate with the United States — are not relevant. People openly say that was at a time when China had the Soviet Union as an enemy, China needed the United States for technology and for capital. China also needed the United States for World Trade Organization (WTO) membership, and now China has all of those things. So the great discontinuity is more likely to be from the Chinese rather than from the United States.

RUDYARD GRIFFITHS: So, David, that poses a vital question for your side of the motion, which is, will China push on certain red lines?

DAVID LI: Well, my observation is that the Chinese side is willing to work on these difficult issues. The Chinese side has always said that, and we are not making new claims. We are willing to work with multiple parties.

However, we are not willing to work with interventionist American policy. The essence of the problem is that after the global financial crisis, the confidence level went down in the United States. As a result, the United States has been giving China mixed signals, even though the White House has been very clear in its policy. The Congress, as well as the candidates for the U.S. presidency, have been giving very mixed signals, and many Chinese people do not fully understand American politics. So the Chinese take this as a signal that the outside world is becoming more and more hostile toward Chinese economic and political emergence. That is the issue.

I would suggest that people in the West try to understand the issues, try to put these relatively small issues in a larger context, and try to understand that the Chinese side is not changing its position. The West has to solve its problems, starting with their financial challeges, and then, when the West is more confident, it will be easier for China to work with them.

NIALL FERGUSON: You may not have heard the voice of Chinese power before, ladies and gentlemen. This is what it sounds like. Get used to it! Because this is the kind of firm, self-confident, and more assertive China that I have seen more and more, of during my trips to China and in my encounters with Chinese academics and statesmen in recent years.

Going right back to the question, does the United States have the option of drawing lines anywhere in Asia in the way that it did during the Eisenhower administration or indeed during the days of the Nixon administration? I don't think so. And the reason I don't think so relates to David's point. Where are the resources? Look at the Congressional Budget Office projections of where the United States is going to be. I don't know if you saw Jim Baker's article in the *Wall Street Journal*.[9] He concluded that in nine years, the United States will be spending more on the interest on the federal debt than on national security.

The Congressional Budget Office has projections for what the United States would save if it reduced its overseas troop presence to 30,000. Thirty thousand! Now in that world — and we are racing toward that world in this decade — the idea that the United States can say to China, this far and no further, and adopt a realpolitik, a balance of power policy with a threat of military action, well, that idea becomes less and less plausible. And that's precisely the point of this debate. It's the way that power shifts. It's somewhat imperceptible but when it shifts, ladies and gentlemen, it talks a little bit like David.

RUDYARD GRIFFITHS: So, ladies and gentlemen, I'm now going to call on our debaters for their closing arguments. They're each going to be given three minutes to make their case to try to sway any final undecided votes. We're going to have our closing remarks in the opposite order of our opening statements. So, Dr. Kissinger, if you could please begin.

---

[9]   James A. Baker, "How to Deal with the Debt Limit," *Wall Street Journal*, June 17, 2011.

HENRY KISSINGER: The issue is not whether or not China will grow in magnitude. That will clearly happen. The issue is twofold. First, how China uses its growing capacities, and secondly, whether the United States and its allies are willing to adjust to the new international environment. I see nothing organic in the situation that leads me to believe that China will dominate the 21st century. China will play a larger role in the 21st century.

The challenge is whether America can redefine itself after its century of progress, and similarly, how China redefines itself when it absorbs its economic growth. I believe the United States has the capacity to draw lines, but we have to be selective in drawing the lines. More than that, we should try to move toward a relationship in which the lines that separate us are not the crucial element, but the things we do together.

RUDYARD GRIFFITHS: David Li, your three minutes, please.

DAVID LI: Let me start by reiterating a remark which I made in my opening statement. That is that the changes which have been going on in China for the past three decades at most are only halfway done. The country is still changing. We still have gas in our gas tank. The changes will be more than economic. The changes will also be societal and political. Also, I would like to remind you that the destination of China's emergence is not world dominance. By no means does China want to dominate the world. There is only one dominant country in the world: that is the United States. It is not the dream, not the aspiration of China, not the capacity of China, to emulate the success of the United States in the dominance of the world. It is simply not in the genes of our Confucian tradition.

That being understood, I urge you to think about a different perspective. Forget about the past five hundred years of Western philosophy, of Western perspective. Forget about looking at international relations in terms of winners and losers. Instead, look through the lens of traditional Chinese philosophers, the Confucians. The Confucians advocated for a harmonious world in which individuals are at peace with the outside world, and with each other, and countries are working with each other to solve international conflicts. I urge you to consider this perspective to understand the ongoing changes in the Chinese economy and society.

Finally, let me call upon you to have patience and to understand that we are not bystanders, we are participants. When we become hostile, when we worry about China's emergence, when we worry about the relative decline of the United States, or the decline of the West, we create problems for the world, we provoke negative, suspicious forces in China. Indeed, this world could become a very uncomfortable world. So in the end I urge you to think about these issues again. China's emergence does not imply that China will dominate the world. The 21st century will belong to China and also will belong to any countries, any nations or peoples who are willing to follow the flow. Together we all will own the century. Thank you.

RUDYARD GRIFFITHS: Fareed Zakaria, you're next.

FAREED ZAKARIA: We are going through a crisis of confidence in the Western world, and this has been true when we have been faced with these kinds of new and different challenges and when we have faced nations that seem to be on the rise and on the march. George Kennan, the great American statesman and writer,[10] used to write routinely about how he thought the United States would never be able to withstand the Soviet challenge, because we were weak and fickle and we changed our minds and they were far-sighted and strategic. We were tactical and stupid. Yet somehow it worked out all right. There is a tendency to think the same of China — that they have this incredible long-term vision and that Americans are bumbling idiots.

There is a wonderful story that encapsulates this: Zhou Enlai is supposed to have said, I think actually in a conversation with Henry Kissinger, when asked what he thought of the French Revolution, "It's too soon to tell." And everyone thought, oh, my goodness, he's a genius, he is so far-sighted, he thinks in centuries. Well, it turns out he meant — this was in 1973 — the French revolution of 1968, the student revolution. And it was perfectly rational at that point to say that it was too soon to tell.

So don't believe that the Chinese are strategic masterminds and the United States are bumbling. We have

---

[10] George F. Kennan (1904–2005), American diplomat, political scientist, and historian. Called "the father of containment" for his advocacy of that policy in U.S. relations with the Soviet Union.

managed to bumble our way through a rather advanced position despite the challenges from the Kaiser's Germany, from the Soviet Union, from Nazi Germany, and I think what you will find is that the United States — North America, even — are creating an extraordinary model in this new world. We are becoming the first universal nation, a country that draws people from all parts of the world, people of all colours, creeds, and religions, and finds a way to harness their talent and build a kind of universal dream. It happens here, and it draws together people from all over the world.

Look at this panel: three of the people on this panel, Niall Ferguson, myself, and Henry Kissinger, are immigrants who've come and found their fortune in the United States because it welcomed the most talented people in the world and allowed them to flourish in whatever they wanted, even to denounce the United States, as Niall Ferguson is now doing. So I urge you to think about this: if we lose faith in ourselves, if we lose faith in the power of free and open societies, we do more damage than anything else we could do. We need to fix our economy, yes. We need to fix all these things. The Congressional Budget Office used to predict that we were going to pay off our debt in fifteen years, and that was ten years ago. Now they predict that we are going to be immiserated. We'll see how it works. My point is — don't lose faith in free and open societies, vote with your heart.

RUDYARD GRIFFITHS: Niall, your final, closing remarks, please.

NIALL FERGUSON: Well, ladies and gentlemen, we've heard that China is likely to repeat the experience of other Asian countries, and run out of steam, maybe. But thus far it has done far better than these other Asian countries. China has achieved the biggest and fastest industrial revolution of them all, lifting hundreds of millions of people out of poverty. I don't agree with David. I think this story isn't half over. It's maybe a quarter over. There's a lot more still to come.

The second point I want to make to you is that the West's problems are far more serious than we have just heard from Fareed. And one of the biggest problems is that kind of complacency. As we speak, the Eurozone is falling apart, an experiment with a single currency is disintegrating mainly because of the insolvency of the cradle of democracy, Greece. As we speak, the public finances of the United States are — if you do the math, which I do — more or less in the same position as they were in Greece two years ago. The trajectory of the debt is not different. It may only be a matter of time before a fiscal crisis strikes the United States, the magnitude of which we will never have seen before.

You know what? If we'd had this debate a hundred years ago, and the motion had been that the 20th century would belong to the United States, who would have voted for it? It would have seemed, certainly to any British debater, preposterous. A British debater would have said, "Those Yanks, with their trivially small military forces . . . Yeah, they have a big economy, but look at all their social problems. Look at the squalor and poverty in their cities. It would have been very easy to make the case in 1911 that America would falter as we've heard China will falter during this debate. And yet it happened. Economic power came first, and then geopolitical power.

I want to conclude with a quotation. "What if China gradually expands its economic ties, acts calmly and moderately, and slowly enlarges its sphere of influence, seeking only greater friendship and influence in the world? What if it quietly positions itself as the alternative to a hectoring and arrogant America? How will America cope? This is a new challenge for the United States, one for which it is largely unprepared." They are the words of Fareed Zakaria, ladies and gentlemen. And that is precisely why China will own the 21st century, and you should vote for this motion.

RUDYARD GRIFFITHS: This was an exceedingly hard-fought and well-contested debate, and let me reiterate something that Peter Munk has said of past Munk Debates. It's one thing for any one of these individuals to get up on a stage in front of an audience and give a set-piece speech. It's something quite different to have this sparring, this meeting of minds, and to do it with the eloquence and conviction that our debaters have shown during this debate.

One final comment, Dr. Kissinger: I think you have denied your public some very special talents that you've had in waiting until your eighty-eighth year to engage in a public debate. You were absolutely outstanding, sir. Thank you.

Summary: At evening's start, the pre-debate vote was 39 percent in favour of the resolution and 40 percent against, and 21 percent were undecided. The final vote showed a shift and a disappearance of the undecided voters, with 38 percent in favour of the resolution and 62 percent against.

HENRY KISSINGER IN CONVERSATION WITH
JOHN GEIGER

JOHN GEIGER: I've just finished reading your book *On China.* It's fascinating reading, and it had me wondering whether the ancient Chinese strategy of "five baits for barbarian management" [a Han dynasty practice of lavishing clothes, carriages, fine food, music, slaves, etc. on invaders in order to 'corrupt' them] is still being practised today?

HENRY KISSINGER: To some extent, yes. I frankly don't remember what all the five baits are; it was put forward in the 19th century when Europeans were beginning to invade China, but it harkens back to more ancient Chinese tradition. The fundamental difference between the Chinese and Western approach to strategy is that the Western approach is aimed at the capability of the other side; the Chinese is aimed at the psychology of the other side. So they pay a lot of attention to intangibles of hospitality, forms of dealing with the interlocutor.

JOHN GEIGER: Economic power and geopolitical influence often go hand in hand.

HENRY KISSINGER: But not always. For example, you take Saudi Arabia — that's a lot of economic power, but not a conventional geopolitical influence.

JOHN GEIGER: In 2020 China will have surpassed the United States' GDP, so with this in mind why wouldn't the following eighty years of this century belong to China?

HENRY KISSINGER: For one thing, the Chinese have to distribute that GDP to a lot more people than the United States. They have to distribute it among 1.3 billion people, so that the per capita income of China will be considerably below the per capita income of the United States. So many of the indices that people cite, like the Chinese have better high-speed trains — well, that means Chinese travellers are more comfortable than American travellers insofar as they use railways. But it doesn't necessarily translate into international influence.

There are many other aspects to international influence which have to do with the structure of diplomacy. So I do not think it is at all foreordained that China will be the dominant country. And, in fact, I would go a step further. I would say we have to get to the point where the issue of dominance does not overshadow the whole relationship. Because neither side will be able to achieve dominance, and the effort to achieve it might lead to clashes that undermine the whole international system.

JOHN GEIGER: Arising from that, will China only be an economic challenger to the United States? You refer to clashes. Is it also possible there will be cultural or military challenges?

HENRY KISSINGER: I think China will certainly be an economic competitor. It will almost certainly, and I would say certainly, have its own political view on international affairs. I would like to think that a potential military clash is way down the list of priorities, and that the leaders of both sides can get to a state of mind where they can fundamentally exclude that from their relationship.

JOHN GEIGER: The United States has such tremendous soft power advantages in the world. Its ability to sell its value system abroad. Obviously its immense cultural impact globally. Can you see China ever challenging the United States in those respects?

HENRY KISSINGER: No. I think the structure of the Chinese language, and even the current structure of Chinese technology, makes this a very forbidding objective for China, that they should outdo us in soft power. It's one of the reasons why I don't accept the proposition that the next century will belong to China. All the inventions of soft power, Facebook, Google, Twitter, they all came from the United States. Of the leading twenty-five universities in the world, I think only one of them is Chinese, and the vast majority are American. So in terms of creative potential, the United States still has huge assets.

JOHN GEIGER: Can China and the United States manage the world in the 21st century, or is it going to be much more of a multipolar world; are they the only two key players?

HENRY KISSINGER: No. China and the United States should be in close consultation, and they should not drift into a position of confrontation. But they should also avoid the impression that they are trying to run the world, because there are other countries of great magnitude — for example, India — which should play a role. But the world is now so multipolar, and the issues are so global, that any attempt by two countries, no matter how powerful, to impose their preferences would create a reaction on the part of the others that would defeat its own objective.

JOHN GEIGER: You have seen so much of the world and seen the world change obviously tremendously since you were secretary of state. Do you think it's a better world today than it was when you were in that position?

HENRY KISSINGER: It's such a different world from the world forty years ago. Of course there were no comput-ers when I was in office. There were no cell phones. I had a radio in my car so in an emergency I could be reached, but the whole world would be reached with me. When I wrote my memoirs thirty years ago, my office did it on carbon paper. Video conferences were unknown. So I could go on and on and on.

Some of the structure of the problem of how you relate across continents to each other, that has remained the same. Is it a better world? In the ability to collect information, there is a reach now that would have been totally out of imagination thirty or forty years ago. In the ability to synthesize what you already know, it may be precisely because you have everything at your fingertips by pressing a button that the ability to train your mind to do long-range thinking may decline. So we are now in a totally new period in human history.

JOHN GEIGER: In your experience, does Canada have a profile in China distinct from the United States, or how is Canada viewed with respect to China?

HENRY KISSINGER: My impression is that China looks at Canada as a country with which it can have strong economic relations, because they can make acquisitions here with less fear of being used for political purposes. At the same time I would assume that the Chinese, on political issues, group in their mind Canada more with the United States than with themselves, almost certainly.

JOHN GEIGER: When you first made this very critical breakthrough in terms of the United States' relationship with China, were you aware of Prime Minister Pierre

Trudeau's overtures to China? Did Canada's early connection —

HENRY KISSINGER: Well, actually, as it happened, Trudeau was a friend of mine, or at least somebody I regarded highly, and since I was a professor once, he treated me in a friendlier way than he treated other American officials. So I knew that China was on his mind, but for us, as Americans, as a country, the problem was different than for Canada. For us it would be a reversal of a long-held policy, but I knew that Trudeau would welcome what we did. I had frequent contact with Trudeau, even after he left office, especially after he left office.

JOHN GEIGER: Do you think that an equivalent of the current Arab Spring is possible in China, or likely in Asia?

HENRY KISSINGER: First of all, we have to see what the Arab Spring produces. Is it possible that there could be riots or demonstrations — we see it every month almost, because the process of economic change in China produces people with grievances, that's inevitable. I don't expect an outbreak of the magnitude of the Arab Spring.

JOHN GEIGER: Is that for cultural reasons, reasons of the Chinese culture, or are there fewer grievances?

HENRY KISSINGER: There are grievances, but there may be cause to believe that not by democratic means but over time they will be met. In any event, even the current

Chinese prime minister has pointed out that some political reforms are essential.

DAVID LI IN CONVERSATION WITH JOHN GEIGER

JOHN GEIGER: In your opinion, is China likely to only ever be an economic challenger to the United States and to the West, or is there a possibility as well that it will become a cultural challenger?

DAVID LI: Well, "challenger" is the wrong word. I strongly disagree with the usage of the word challenger. China's economic emergence actually provides overall newer and more business opportunities for people in the rest of the world. Of course, I understand that China's economic emergence will also mean a painful adjustment process for some people, like the shoemakers in North Carolina, or maybe some steelworkers in Chicago or Illinois. That is a job that domestic governments in the United States and Canada, perhaps, will have to do. We are facing a global change in the landscape of the economy. So overall, it's a positive force; however, it does require other parties to make some internal adjustments. That's the economics. On the political side, I don't think that China's economic and political emergence will be a challenge to the U.S. dominance.

JOHN GEIGER: What about military?

DAVID LI: I don't think so. We have to go back into history to understand the origin of Chinese change so far in the past three decades. We have to go back to the years as early as 170 years ago. At that time, the world witnessed a spectacular clash between two civilizations. The traditional Chinese inward-looking, not so innovative culture and civilization against the very adventurous, very innovative, and sometimes aggressive Western culture. And that was no game — total failure for the Chinese culture, and the Chinese government of that time, which came down, even today, as a big humiliation and which caused actions, reactions, the overreactions on the Chinese part. So the energy of today's Chinese change, or progress, comes from these humiliations.

The dream has never been to seek revenge. The dream has never been to seek to ameliorate the dominance of the United States in the world. Rather it is to revive — revive the respect, the status, and the self-contented nature of the old Chinese civilization, for example in the Tang Dynasty. So it's not a challenge to the United States; it's more about a new pattern of collaboration in global affairs with the United States and other countries.

JOHN GEIGER: Do you think an equivalent to the Arab Spring that we're seeing in the Middle East will eventually also affect Asia, and China — the sorts of demands from individuals for an opening, more democracy, improved and enhanced human rights? Will that likely affect China?

DAVID LI: Well, with economic development, with improvements in living standards, it is natural, it is good, that people are demanding more freedom in expressing themselves, more freedom in participating in public issues and decisions. That's natural. That has been there despite any developments outside China. This is good. And these will to some extent — and is perhaps inevitable down the road in the coming two or three years — create some tensions, social tensions, and maybe even some small problems in certain regions in China, certain areas in China. That, I think, is fully understood by many people in China.

However, if you push people hard, if you push the young kids hard, if you tell them the big picture, which is to just talk about the past 170 years of change, they realize that China finally is on the path of revival, and this path in general is in the direction of giving people more freedom. It should not be undermined, it should not go back. So people understand, people have patience, people are looking at the changes upcoming. So I don't see major problems down the road. I see a general trend of continued change, although I do believe there will be minor social issues or even uprisings in local regions.

JOHN GEIGER: Can China and the United States dominate in the 21st century? Are we likely to see more of a multipolar world, a world of coequals?

DAVID LI: I would say the world is changing; the dominance of the United States, arguably and most likely, is the past. In the new world there will be multiple forces, including the Chinese economic and political voices. So we're in a new world, and China is definitely not looking for dominance, not looking for dominance together with the United States; it's not in the cultural gene, it's not in the tradition of the Chinese Confucianist ideology. It's more about maintaining stable domestic issues — deal with domestic issues, and then, based on that, co-operate and work with others. That's the Chinese perspective on these issues.

So far, China has been trying to help, trying to co-operate with countries in the world, including the United States during the financial crisis, for example. In the past two years, China has not sold huge volumes of U.S. Treasury bonds despite the current debate of the ceiling, of lifting the ceiling of the Treasury bond — China's government is not selling its holding of Treasury bonds. And also during the height of the financial crisis, the renminbi did not depreciate against the U.S. dollar. It's a fact. Many other currencies depreciated against the U.S. dollar during the height of the financial crisis. So this shows the attitude of co-operation, of understanding. So I think both sides have to work together, and there's a hope that we will be in a co-operative and a multipolar world.

JOHN GEIGER: One of the most successful consumer products of the last decade has been the iPhone. It has obviously revolutionized the way people interact with each other and their devices. It's manufactured in China, but its development came about in the United States, of course. China obviously is a great economic power in its capacity to manufacture, but can it innovate in a way that Apple's Steve Jobs, and Apple Corporation, have been able to do? Is that also in the DNA of China?

DAVID LI: Well, in general, I would say you have to be patient. China's economic emergence is only thirty-three years old. For a large country it has made progress [compared to] Western countries, perhaps in the last 150 years. It's already huge progress, and innovation takes time. Innovation takes years of education of young people, it takes years of establishment of supporting institutions such as venture capital, private equity, so on and so forth. This is gradually coming.

I do see among our students that urge to innovate, that urge to establish corporations like Apple, like Microsoft. So I do think, in general, innovation is coming in China, but we have to be patient. That being said, I would speculate that in China we may have a very different model of innovation, due to the nature of the management of the society and economy. That is, the most innovative, revolutionary products will continue to come from the United States, where some very creative, even crazy entrepreneurs can freely express themselves, can grow up. Whereas in China we may not have that kind of soil for these kinds of crazy, extremely innovative people. That's the nature of the two systems.

So down the road China may provide an alternative model of social management in which, relatively speaking, more weight is put on social well-being, social stability, rather than on individual liberty, whereas in the United States we have the opposite system. So the relative advantage of the U.S. system is to be extremely innovative. Meanwhile, don't forget, one of the costs of [the] extreme form of innovation in the United States is also, maybe, a large number of people who may be left behind. So the extreme amount of inequality, or whatever you measure, will also be there. They are two alternative models; the two countries provide two extremes for other countries to learn from, to study.

JOHN GEIGER: Increasingly nations are understanding the importance of soft power. This is obviously something the United States does very, very well. The way in which it distributes its culture internationally, and the way in which its values become global values. Is China likely to ever fulfill a similar role internationally? Can you see China using soft power eventually in the same way the United States does?

DAVID LI: Well, I would say that China's soft powers certainly will increase. The influence of China certainly will increase. The very fact of the Munk Debate focusing on the future of China — the very fact of me, coming from China, being invited to this very important event, and being interviewed by you — is a reflection of the relative increase of China's influence in the world.

That being said, I should emphasize, it is not the explicit objective of Chinese intellectuals and government to enhance, and to compete with the United States in, the area of soft power. Soft power will gradually increase when China handles its own domestic affairs properly. By doing that, it provides a kind of role model for many of the poor fellows in the world to say, look, this is a viable model for us resource-constrained, extremely poor countries to modernize. So through that, China will have more soft power. It's not through building up military dominance, it is not through expressly making movies, expressing the cultural values of a country. Rather it's through deeds, rather through pure voices. It's example.

JOHN GEIGER: How is Canada perceived in China today?

DAVID LI: Canada is perceived very, very positively in China, because being an open-minded culture, being also a rich country in resources, naturally complements the economic needs of China, so that certainly is a positive side. Meanwhile I have to admit that many young people in China cannot fully separate the Canadian culture from the American culture.

JOHN GEIGER: Many Canadians cannot separate the cultures.

DAVID LI: Right, so therefore, inevitably, unfortunately,

the Canadians carry some of the burden of the U.S.-Sino disputes, so I wouldn't blame you, I would perhaps shift the blame to the United States.

JOHN GEIGER: But that perception persists in China, that Canada is too closely aligned with the United States?

DAVID LI: It's increasing — it's increasingly less obvious, because with the large amount of cultural and educational exchanges between the two countries, people in China realize that Canadians are different from Americans, Canada is different from the United States. For example, in China, we have a lot of very super popular comedians — Canadians — they speak Mandarin, they play funny movies and TV shows in China. So through them, people in China, on the street, now gradually know more about Canada.

JOHN GEIGER: We used to export people like Norman Bethune, now we export comedians . . .

DAVID LI: That's right, you mention Norman Bethune. People of my age can mostly, almost all of us, memorize the article written by Chairman Mao in memory of Norman Bethune.[11]

---

[11] Mao Zedong, "In Memory of Norman Bethune," originally written on December 21, 1939. During the Cultural Revolution, Mao's tribute to the Canadian surgeon and his "spirit of absolute selflessness" was required reading in Chinese schools.

ACKNOWLEDGEMENTS

The Munk Debates are the product of the public spirit-edness of a remarkable group of civic-minded organizations and individuals. First and foremost, these debates would not be possible without the vision and leadership of the Aurea Foundation. Founded in 2006 by Peter and Melanie Munk, the Aurea Foundation supports Canadian individuals and institutions involved in the study and development of public policy. The debates are the foundation's signature initiative; a model for the kind of substantive public policy conversation Canadians can foster globally. Since their creation in 2008, the foundation has underwritten the entire cost of each semi-annual debate. The debates have also benefited from the input and advice of members of the advisory board, including Mark Cameron, Andrew Coyne, Devon Cross, Allan Gotlieb, George Jonas, Margaret MacMillan, Anthony Munk, and Janice Stein.

Since their inception the Munk Debates have sought to take the discussions that happen at each event to national and international audiences. Here the debates have benefited immeasurably from a partnership with Canada's national newspaper the *Globe and Mail* and the counsel of its editor-in-chief John Stackhouse.

With the publication of this superb book, House of Anansi Press is helping the debates reach new audiences in Canada and internationally. The debates' organizers would like to thank Anansi Chair, Scott Griffin, and President and Publisher, Sarah MacLachlan, for their enthusiasm for this book project and insights into how to translate the spoken debate into a powerful written intellectual exchange.

ABOUT THE DEBATERS

NIALL FERGUSON is Laurence A. Tisch Professor of History at Harvard and William Ziegler Professor of Business Administration at Harvard Business School. He is also a Senior Research Fellow at Jesus College, Oxford University, and a Senior Fellow at the Hoover Institution, Stanford University. Ferguson is the author of numerous bestsellers, including *The Ascent of Money*. His latest book, *Civilization: The West and the Rest*, will be released in Canada in November 2011. A prolific commentator on contemporary politics and economics, Ferguson is a contributing editor for the *Financial Times* and senior columnist with *Newsweek*.

HENRY KISSINGER was the 56th secretary of state of the United States from 1973 to 1977. He is one of the world's most influential commentators on geopolitics. Among his many accomplishments as a public servant

Dr. Kissinger has been credited for normalizing relations between the United States and China at a crucial juncture in the history of both countries. After leaving government service, he founded Kissinger Associates, an international consulting firm, of which he is chairman. Dr. Kissinger received the Nobel Peace Prize in 1973 and the Presidential Medal of Freedom (America's highest civilian award) in 1977. He is the author of more than a dozen books, including his most recent, *On China*.

DAVID DAOKUI LI is the Director of the Center for China in the World Economy at the Tsinghua University School of Economics and Management in Beijing. He currently teaches courses on economic transition, corporate finance, international economics, and China's economy. Professor Li holds a Ph.D. in economics from Harvard, and is one of three academic members of the monetary policy committee of the central bank of China. Li is a delegate to the Beijing People's Congress and a member of the Chinese People's Political Consultative Committee.

FAREED ZAKARIA is the host of CNN's flagship international affairs program, *Fareed Zakaria: GPS*, and the editor-at-large of *Time* magazine. He is the author of the international bestsellers *The Future of Freedom* and *The Post-American World*. *Esquire* called him "the most influential foreign policy adviser of his generation," and in 2010, *Foreign Policy* named him one of the top 100 global thinkers. Zakaria was the editor of *Newsweek*'s international edition for ten years before joining *Time*. He also spent eight years as managing editor of *Foreign Affairs*.

ABOUT THE EDITORS

RUDYARD GRIFFITHS is a co-host of the Business News Network television show *SqueezePlay* and a columnist for the *National Post*. He is the co-director of the Munk Debates and the Salon Speakers Series. He is a co-founder of the Historica-Dominion Institute, Canada's largest history and civics NGO. In 2006, he was named one of Canada's "Top 40 under 40" by the *Globe and Mail*. He is the editor of twelve books on history, politics, and international affairs, and the author of *Who We Are: A Citizen's Manifesto*, which was a *Globe and Mail* Best Book of 2009 and a finalist for the Shaughnessy Cohen Prize for Political Writing. He lives in Toronto.

PATRICK LUCIANI is the co-director of the Munk Debates and the Salon Speakers Series. He was a former executive director of the Donner Canadian Foundation, and he has authored two books on economic issues. He is also

a senior resident at Massey College and the co-author of
XXL: Obesity and the Limits of Shame with Neil Seeman.
He lives in Toronto.

ABOUT THE MUNK DEBATES

The Munk Debates are Canada's premier public policy event. Held semi-annually, the debates provide leading thinkers with a global forum to discuss the major public policy issues facing the world and Canada. Each event takes place in Toronto in front of a live audience, and the proceedings are covered by domestic and international media. Participants in recent Munk Debates include Robert Bell, Tony Blair, John Bolton, Paul Collier, Howard Dean, Hernando de Soto, Gareth Evans, Mia Farrow, Niall Ferguson, William Frist, David Gratzer, Rick Hillier, Christopher Hitchens, Richard Holbrooke, Henry Kissinger, Charles Krauthammer, Lord Nigel Lawson, Stephen Lewis, David Li, Bjørn Lomborg, Elizabeth May, George Monbiot, Dambisa Moyo, Samantha Power, and Fareed Zakaria. The Munk Debates are a project of the Aurea Foundation; a charitable organization established in 2006 by philanthropists

Peter and Melanie Munk to promote public policy research and discussion. For more information visit www.munkdebates.com.

PERMISSIONS

Permission is gratefully acknowledged to reprint excerpts from the following:

(p. 59–65) "Henry Kissinger in Conversation," by John Geiger. Copyright 2011, *Globe and Mail.* Reprinted with permission.

(p. 67–74) "David Li in Conversation," by John Geiger. Copyright 2011, *Globe and Mail.* Reprinted with permission.

Also available

Hitchens vs. Blair
Edited by Rudyard Griffiths

ISBN: 978-1-77089-008-4

Two formidable minds. One powerfully charged debate.

On November 26, 2010, intellectual juggernaut and staunch atheist Christopher Hitchens went head-to-head with former British prime minister Tony Blair, one of the Western world's most openly devout political leaders, on the highly charged topic of religion. Few world leaders have had a greater hand in shaping current events than Blair; few writers have been more outspoken and polarizing than Hitchens. In this edition of The Munk Debates — Canada's premier international debate series — Hitchens and Blair square off on the contentious questions that continue to dog the topic of religion in our globalized world: How does faith influence our actions? What is the role of people of faith in the public sphere? Is religious doctrine rigid, or should we allow for flexibility in our interpretations?

For the first time ever, this exclusive debate, which played out to a sold-out audience, is now available in print form, along with candid interviews with Hitchens and Blair. Sharp, provocative, and thoroughly engrossing, *Hitchens vs. Blair* is a rigorous and electrifying intellectual sparring match on the oldest question — Is religion a force for good in the world?

Available in fine bookstores and at www.anansi.ca.
Also available as an e-book.

Also available

The Munk Debates: Volume One
Edited by Rudyard Griffiths
Introduction by Peter Munk

ISBN 978-0-88784-248-1

Launched in 2008 by philanthropists Peter and Melanie Munk, the Munk Debates is Canada's premier international debate series, a highly anticipated cultural event that brings together the world's brightest minds.

This volume includes the first five debates in the series, and features twenty leading thinkers and doers arguing for or against provocative resolutions that address pressing public policy concerns, such as the future of global security, the implications of humanitarian intervention, the effectiveness of foreign aid, the threat of climate change, and the state of health care in Canada and the United States.

Intelligent, informative, and entertaining, *The Munk Debates* is a feast of ideas that captures the prevailing moods, clashing opinions, and most imperative issues of our time.

Available in fine bookstores and at www.anansi.ca.
Also available as an e-book.